# Sculpture

Sue Nicholson

QED Publishing

First published in the UK in 2005 by
QED Publishing
A Quarto Group company
226 City Road
London EC1V 2TT

www.qed-publishing.co.uk



A Catalogue record for this book is available from the British Library.

ISBN 1 84538 416 4

Written by Sue Nicholson
Designed by Susi Martin
Photographer Michael Wicks
Editor Paul Manning

Publisher Steve Evans
Creative Director Louise Morley
Editorial Manager Jean Coppendale

The author and publisher would like to thank:
Billy and Dylan
Sarah Morley for making the models
Ella Slater for the sculptures and Sue Nicholson for the photographs on pages 6–7

Printed and bound in China

## Note to teachers and parents

The projects in this book are aimed at children at Key Stage I and are presented in order of difficulty, from easy to more challenging. Each can be used as a stand-alone activity or as part of another area of study.

While the ideas in the book are offered as inspiration, children should always be encouraged to work from their own imagination and first-hand observations.

All projects in this book require adult supervision.

## Sourcing ideas

★ Encourage the children to source ideas from their own experiences as well as from books, magazines, the Internet, galleries or museums.
★ Prompt them to talk about different types of art they have seen at home or on holiday.
★ Use the 'Click for Art!' boxes as a starting point for finding useful material on the Internet.*
★ Suggest that each child keeps a sketchbook of their ideas.

## Evaluating work

★ Encourage the children to share their work and talk about their ideas and ways of working. What do they like best/least about it? If they did it again, what would they do differently?
★ Help the children to judge the originality of their work and to appreciate the different qualities in others' work. This will help them to value ways of working that are different from their own
★ Encourage the children by displaying their work.

* Website information is correct at the time of going to press. However, the publishers cannot accept liability for information or links found on third-party websites.

# Contents

Words in bold, **like this**, are explained in the Glossary on page 24.

# Getting started

A sculpture is a **three-dimensional** (**3D**) model. This book shows you how to make different kinds of sculpture, from a **clay** pot to a glittery hanging mobile. Here are some of the things you will need to get started.

## Top tip

Always ask first before you use something to make a sculpture!

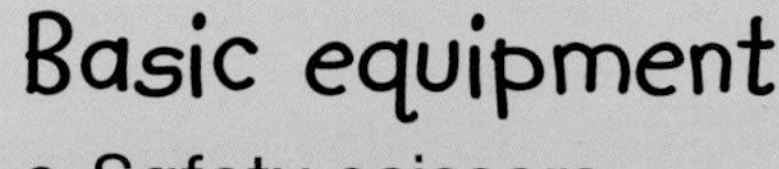

## Basic equipment

- Safety scissors
- Sticky tape
- Felt-tip pens
- Pencils and ruler
- Poster/acrylic paints and brushes
- **PVA** or other white glue

You will also need some extra things which are listed separately for each project.

### Paper

For many of the models you will need thick white paper or thin card. You may also like to use:

- coloured paper
- tissue paper
- **sugar paper**

## Take care!

**Some projects involve cutting and photocopying. Always ask an adult for help where you see this sign:** ⚠

## Top tip

Don't forget to spread out some newspaper to work on, and wear an apron or an old shirt to keep your clothes clean.

### Cardboard

Start a collection of cardboard boxes to use in your sculptures. Look out for:

- cereal packets
- toilet roll or kitchen roll tubes
- large grocery boxes
- egg boxes

## Bits and bobs

Keep a box of things with an interesting **texture** or shape to decorate your sculptures. For example:

- ★ Shells, dried beans and seeds
- ★ String, wool, ribbon and embroidery thread
- ★ Sequins, buttons and beads
- ★ Nails, screws, paperclips and washers
- ★ Tin foil and bottle tops

# Nature sculpture

Have fun making outdoor sculptures from smooth stones, fallen flowers and leaves, twigs, moss or feathers. You can find all the things you need for free in parks, woods or fields!

A spiral of tiny pebbles on a flat stone

## Sculpture ideas

Natural materials can make great outdoor sculptures. Here are some ideas to start you off:

- ★ Arrange berries in a pattern on moss.
- ★ Overlap fallen leaves in the shape of a circle or a star.
- ★ Arrange silky flower petals on a stone or a rock.
- ★ Make rows of pebbles or shells on the beach.
- ★ If it has been snowing, make a sculpture out of piled-up snow.
- ★ If it has been raining, trace lines in mud with a sharp stone or a twig, then add a **pattern** of fallen leaves.

## Changing nature

Ask a grown-up to photograph your nature sculpture. Go back to it the next day and take another photograph to show how it has been changed by wind, rain or animals.

**Click for Art!** To see nature sculptures by Andy Goldsworthy, go to **http://ea.pomona.edu/goldsworthyart.html** For more images click on 'Gallery'. Click on a photo for a closer look.

**Colourful petals and leaves on grass**

**Shells arranged in the shape of a star**

# Glittery mobile

A mobile is a sculpture that moves. This glittery hanging mobile is fun to watch as it gently twists and spins.

**1** Ask an adult to help you cut two pieces of wood dowelling, each about 30cm long.

### You will need:

- Two lengths of wood dowelling
- Cellophane or food wrap
- A thick knitting needle
- String or clear nylon line
- Glitter

### Top tip

To add sound to your sparkly mobile, fix tiny bells to the end of some of the glitter curls.

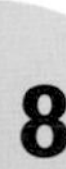

**2** Arrange the two pieces of wood in a cross shape and tie them together at the centre with string.

**3** Spread out a sheet of cellophane on a flat surface. Tape it down at each corner.

**4** Squeeze out some glue, then use a strip of cardboard to shape it into thick blobs with long swirling tails.

**5** Sprinkle different-coloured glitter on the glue, then leave it to dry.

**6** Carefully peel the glitter curls from the cellophane. Make a small hole in the top of each one with a thick knitting needle.

**7** Tie the glitter curls onto the wood with string or clear nylon line. Hang up the mobile and watch it twist and twirl in the breeze!

**Click for Art!**

To see an interactive virtual mobile, go to **www.nga.gov/kids/zone/zone.htm** and click on 'Mobile'.

# Thumb pot

This project shows you how to make a simple clay pot and decorate it with lively colours and patterns.

1 Roll the clay into a ball between the palms of your hands. It should be about half the size of a tennis ball.

2 Holding the ball in one hand, push the thumb of your other hand partway into the middle of the clay.

### You will need:

- Self-hardening modelling clay
- **Modelling tools**

3 Open out the middle of the pot by gently pinching the sides between your thumb and fingers. Keep turning the pot as you pinch, to keep the sides the same thickness.

4 When you are happy with the pot's shape, flatten the bottom by tapping it gently on a flat surface. Leave it to dry out a little, then decorate it using modelling tools or by adding pieces of clay.

**Add simple shapes like this star to decorate your pot**

To see examples of clay pottery, go to **www.thebritishmuseum.ac.uk/compass/** and search for 'clay pot'.

# Decorating your pot

When your clay pot is almost dry, decorate it with a **relief pattern** or press patterns into the side with modelling tools. If you do not have special modelling tools, use:

★ the tip of a pen or pencil
★ a large nail
★ the end of a ruler
★ a blunt metal knife or fork

## Top tip

At Step 2, don't press down too hard with your thumb or you'll make a hole in the bottom of your pot!

**5** When the clay is completely hard, paint your pot with poster paint and leave it to dry. Finish it off with a coat of PVA glue mixed with a little water.

**'Studs' made from flattened balls of clay**

**Long thin sausages of clay stuck on with a little water**

# Clay sculpture

People have been making clay models for thousands of years. For this project, you can use self-hardening modelling clay which does not need to be fired in a **kiln**.

**You will need:**
- Self-hardening modelling clay
- Modelling tools

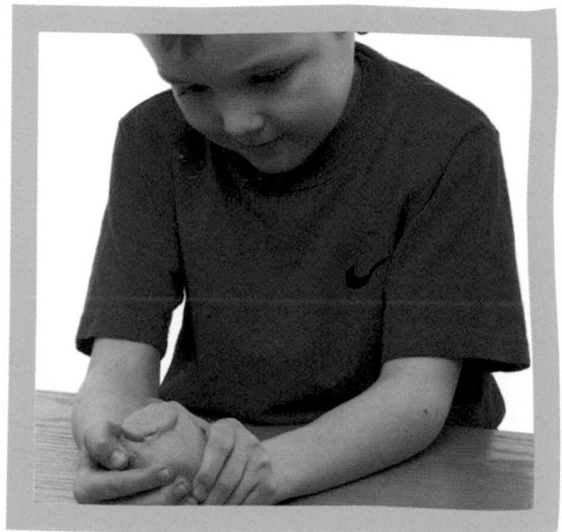

1 Tear off a piece of clay and work it into the shape of a head with your fingers.

2 Add features by sticking on extra bits of clay or cutting it away with a modelling tool. Make hair by squeezing clay through a garlic press so it comes out in long strands.

3 When you are happy with your model, leave the clay to harden.

4 Paint your model with poster paints and leave it to dry.

**Top tip**

Coat your finished model with PVA glue mixed with a little water. The glue looks white at first, but dries to a clear, shiny finish.

**Click for Art!** To see sculptures by Henry Moore, go to **www.henry-moore-fdn.co.uk/** Click on the link to 'Perry Green', then on the interactive map, then on photos of sculptures.

# Animal shapes

Here are some simple animal shapes made out of clay:

# Junk robot

You can make fantastic sculptures out of scrap materials! This robot has been made from cardboard boxes and tubes spray-painted silver.

## You will need:

- A large cardboard box
- Smaller boxes for the robot's lower body, hands and feet
- 9–10 toilet roll tubes
- **Corrugated** cardboard
- Silver spray-paint

1 Glue down the open top of a cardboard box. Ask an adult to help you make a hole in the top and push in a toilet roll tube for the robot's neck. Fix it in place with sticky tape.

2 Glue on a smaller cardboard box to make the lower part of the robot's body. Make two holes underneath and attach toilet roll tubes for the legs.

3 Tape two toilet roll tubes together to make each of the robot's arms. Fix them to the sides of the robot's body with PVA glue.

To see Picasso's 'Head of a Bull', a sculpture made with a bicycle saddle and handlebars, go to **www.artviews.org/cosby.htm** and scroll down.

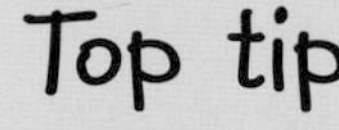

For a shiny metallic look, ask an adult to help you spray your robot with silver paint.

**4** Cut out ears, eyes and a mouth from card and stick them to a small cardboard box to make the robot's head.

**5** Ask an adult to help you cut a hole in the bottom of the head and attach it to the robot's neck.

**6** Glue on feet made from small cardboard boxes. Paint the robot when the glue is dry.

**These robot eyes have been made from an empty egg box**

**Corrugated card mouth**

**Feet made from shaped cardboard boxes**

# Paper sculpture

This colourful bird has been made out of different kinds of paper which have been folded, creased or curled to look three-dimensional.

**You will need:**

- Thick coloured paper
- Scrunched-up newspaper
- A length of ribbon or wool
- A stapler

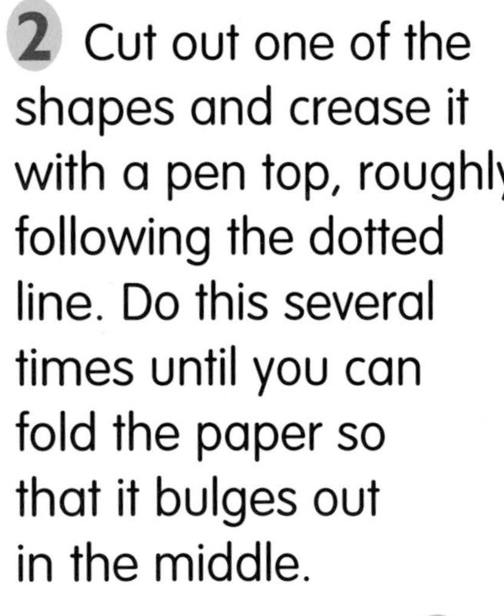

**1** Ask an adult to help you copy and enlarge the bird shape below onto two sheets of thick, brightly coloured paper.

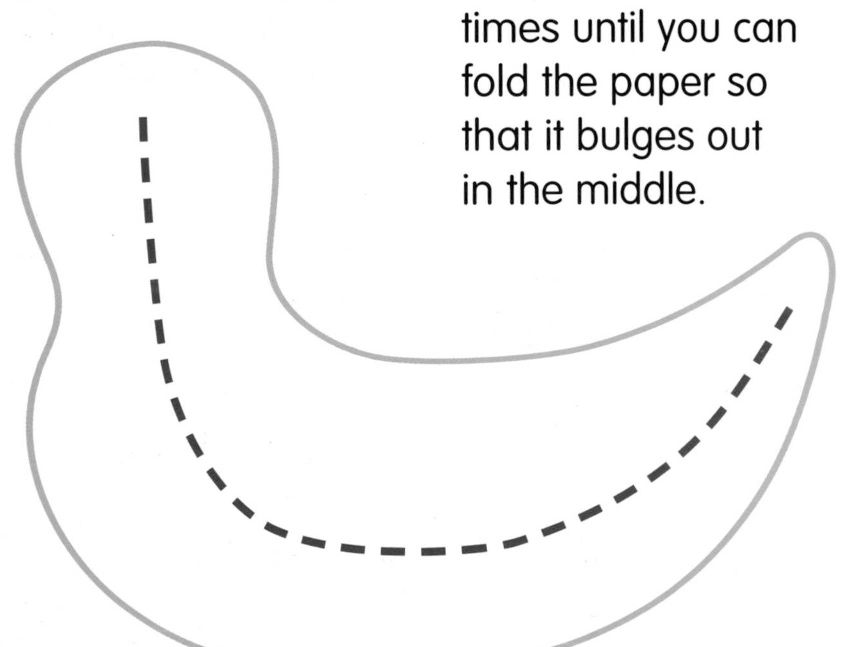

**2** Cut out one of the shapes and crease it with a pen top, roughly following the dotted line. Do this several times until you can fold the paper so that it bulges out in the middle.

**3** Do the same with the other shape, but crease it on the opposite side.

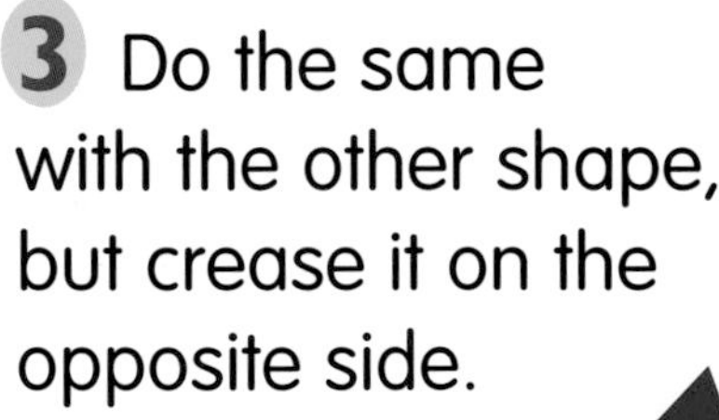

**4** Ask an adult to help you staple the two pieces of paper together so that the sides bulge outwards. Leave a gap at the bird's head and tail, then stuff it with scrunched-up pieces of newspaper.

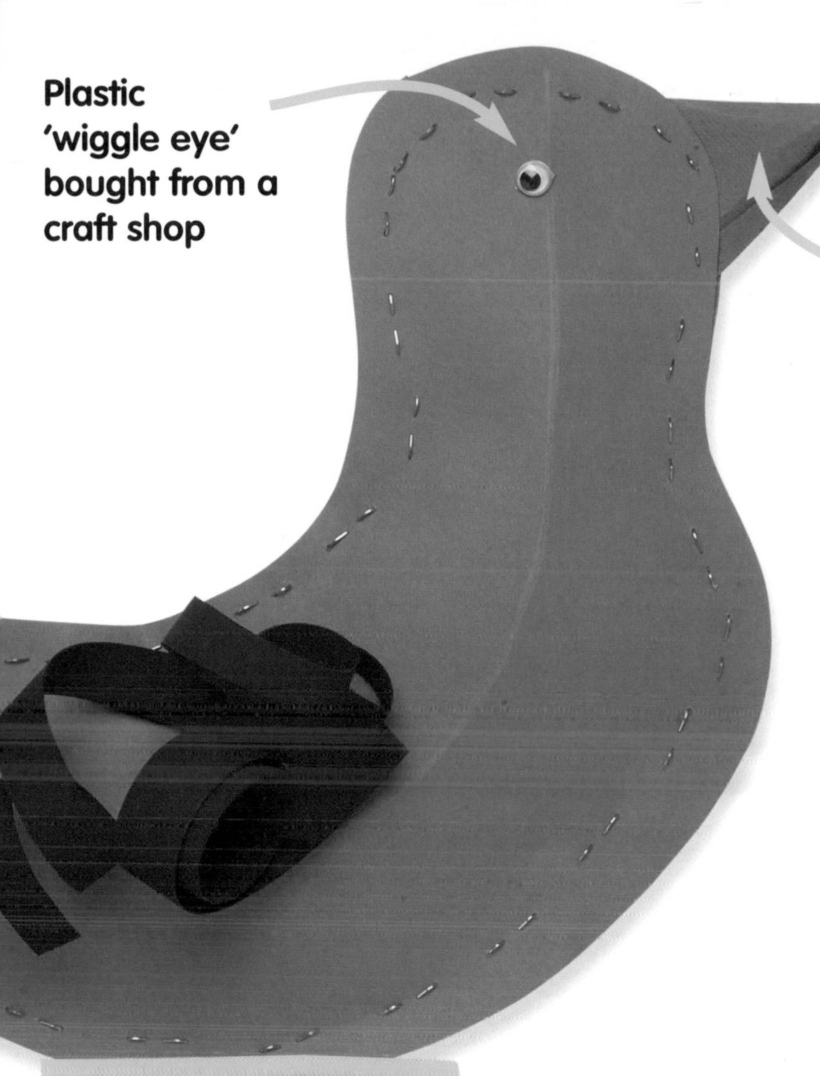

Plastic 'wiggle eye' bought from a craft shop

Card beak folded and glued in a cone shape

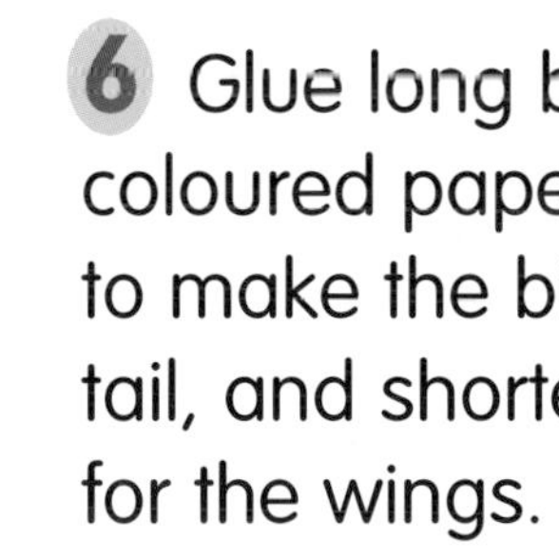

5 Using safety scissors, cut out thin strips of coloured paper and wind them tightly around a pen or pencil so they become curly.

6 Glue long brightly coloured paper curls to make the bird's tail, and shorter curls for the wings.

7 Hang the finished sculpture on the wall with a length of ribbon or wool.

# Paper decorations

1 Cut out 6–10 strips of paper about 3cm wide.

2 Leave two strips 30cm long. Cut two strips 28cm long, and cut two more strips 26cm long.

3 Arrange the strips with the long ones on the outside and the shorter ones in the middle.

4 Staple the strips together at the top and bottom, so that the shape balloons out, then hang it up.

# Cone hats

These simple hats are great to make – and fun to wear!

1 Ask an adult to help you draw a big circle on a sheet of card and cut it out with safety scissors. Cut a straight line from the edge of the circle to the exact centre.

2 Overlap the edges to make a cone shape that fits your head, then stick the edges together with glue or tape.

3 Paint your hat and decorate it with ribbons, sequins or glitter.

4 Ask an adult to help you make a hole in each side of the hat. Cut a piece of elastic or ribbon and tie it through the holes.

### You will need:

- A large sheet of thin cardboard
- Ribbons, sequins, stick-on gems, glitter and feathers for decoration
- A length of elastic or ribbon

**Click for Art!**

To see sculptural hats designed by Pip Hackett, go to **www.vam.ac.uk/collections/fashion/** and search for 'Pip Hackett'.

# Wizard's hat

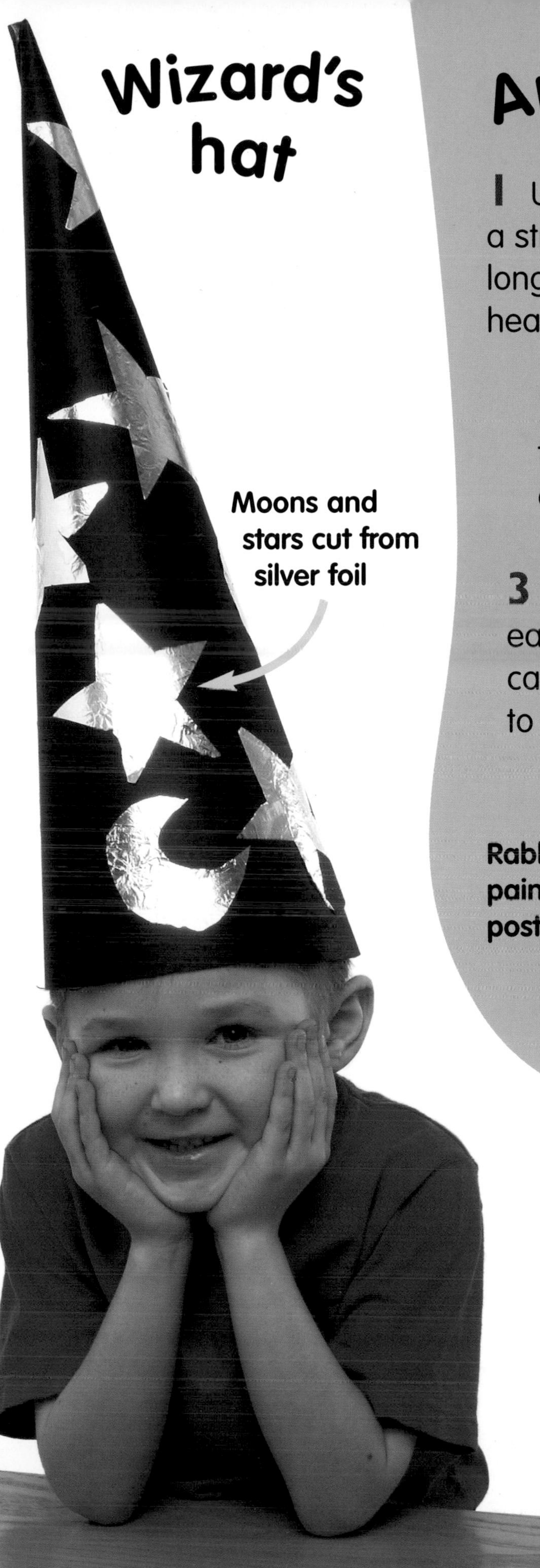

Moons and stars cut from silver foil

# Animal ears

1 Using safety scissors, cut out a strip of cardboard 5cm wide and long enough to go around your head plus an extra 2cm.

2 Fit the strip around your head, then ask an adult to staple the ends of the card together for you.

3 Cut out animal ear shapes from card and glue them to the band.

Rabbit ears painted with poster paints

## Top tip

Try cutting out different-sized circles. The bigger the circle, the wider or taller the hat. The wizard's hat was made from a circle of black card 1m wide.

# Ocean scene

First make and decorate this box for a 3D ocean scene – then turn the page to find out how to fill it with fish and other sea creatures!

1 Cut off the flaps on the open side of the box, or fold them back and glue them to the sides.

You will need:

- A large cardboard box
- Blue cellophane
- Newspaper
- Sandpaper, pebbles and shells

2 Ask an adult to help you cut a rectangular hole in the top of the box to let in light at the back. Paint the box blue inside and out.

3 Glue a piece of blue cellophane underneath the hole in the top of the box to create a watery blue light.

4 Glue sandpaper, small pebbles and shells onto the bottom of your box to make a sandy seabed.

**Click for Art!**

To discover the outdoor sculptures of Oldenburg and van Bruggen:
**www.metmuseum.org/explore/oldenburg/artist.html**

**5** Scrunch up some old newspaper and pack it tightly into a corner of your box. Fix it in place with sticky tape and glue.

**6** Tear more newspaper into strips and glue 2–3 layers over the scrunched-up newspaper, overlapping them as you go.

**7** When the glue is dry, paint the newspaper brown or grey, for rocks.

Now turn the page to find out how to make the sea creatures to put in the box.

# Ocean creatures

Now that you've made the box for your 3D ocean scene, it's time to fill it with colourful fish and sea creatures.

**You will need:**

- Self-hardening modelling clay
- A large plastic bottle
- Glitter glue
- A clear plastic food bag
- Tissue paper
- Clear fishing line

## Clay crab and fishes

Use self-hardening clay to make these sea creatures for your ocean scene.

Have fun decorating your models with bright colours and dotty patterns!

## Plastic bottle fishes

These fish were cut out of a large plastic bottle, then painted with wavy and zigzag patterns.

**Ask an adult to make a hole at the top of your fish, so you can hang it from the top of your box with clear fishing line**

# Plastic bag jellyfish

This sea snail was made from coloured self-hardening clay

This seahorse was made from cardboard, built up with layers of glued newspaper strips, then painted

1 Push some colourful scrunched-up tissue paper into a clear plastic food bag.

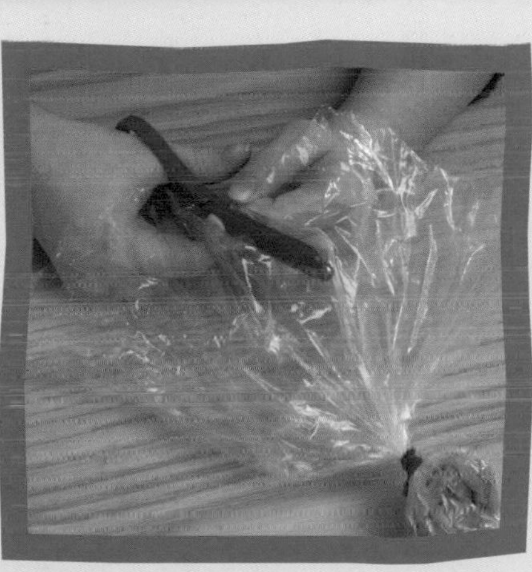

2 Tie the bag around the middle, then cut the open end into strips for the jellyfish's tentacles.

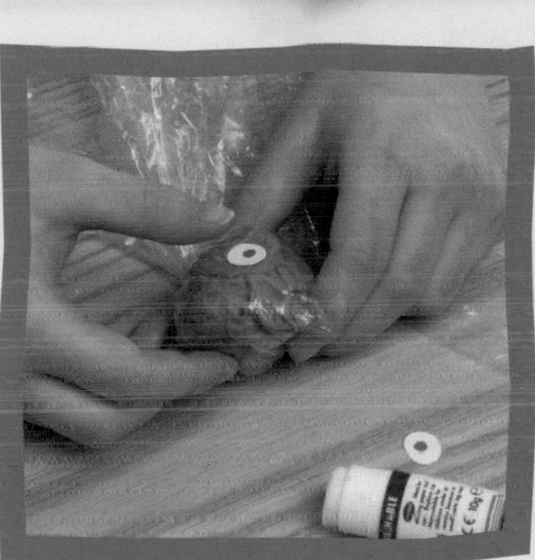

3 Glue on some big cardboard eyes or some 'wiggle eyes' from a craft shop.

**Click for Art!** To design a 3D shape on an interactive art site, go to **www.nga.gov/kids/zone/zone.htm** and click on '3D Twirler'. You may have to download a program to work it.

# Glossary

**clay** a kind of sticky, stretchy earth that can be used to make pots
**corrugated** type of cardboard shaped into folds with a pattern of ridges and grooves
**kiln** large, hot oven used to fire clay to make it last (self-hardening clay does not need to be fired in a kiln)
**modelling tool** special tool made of shaped wood or metal used to sculpt or make patterns in clay
**pattern** the repetition of shape, line or colour in a design
**PVA** strong white glue; can be mixed with water and painted on a model to make it shine
**relief pattern** when part of a pattern sticks out from a background like the pattern on a coin
**sugar paper** thick, textured paper often used in scrapbooks
**texture** the surface or 'feel' of something – for example, rough, soft, furry, bumpy, smooth or velvety
**three-dimensional (3D)** when something has height, width and depth, instead of just being flat

# Index